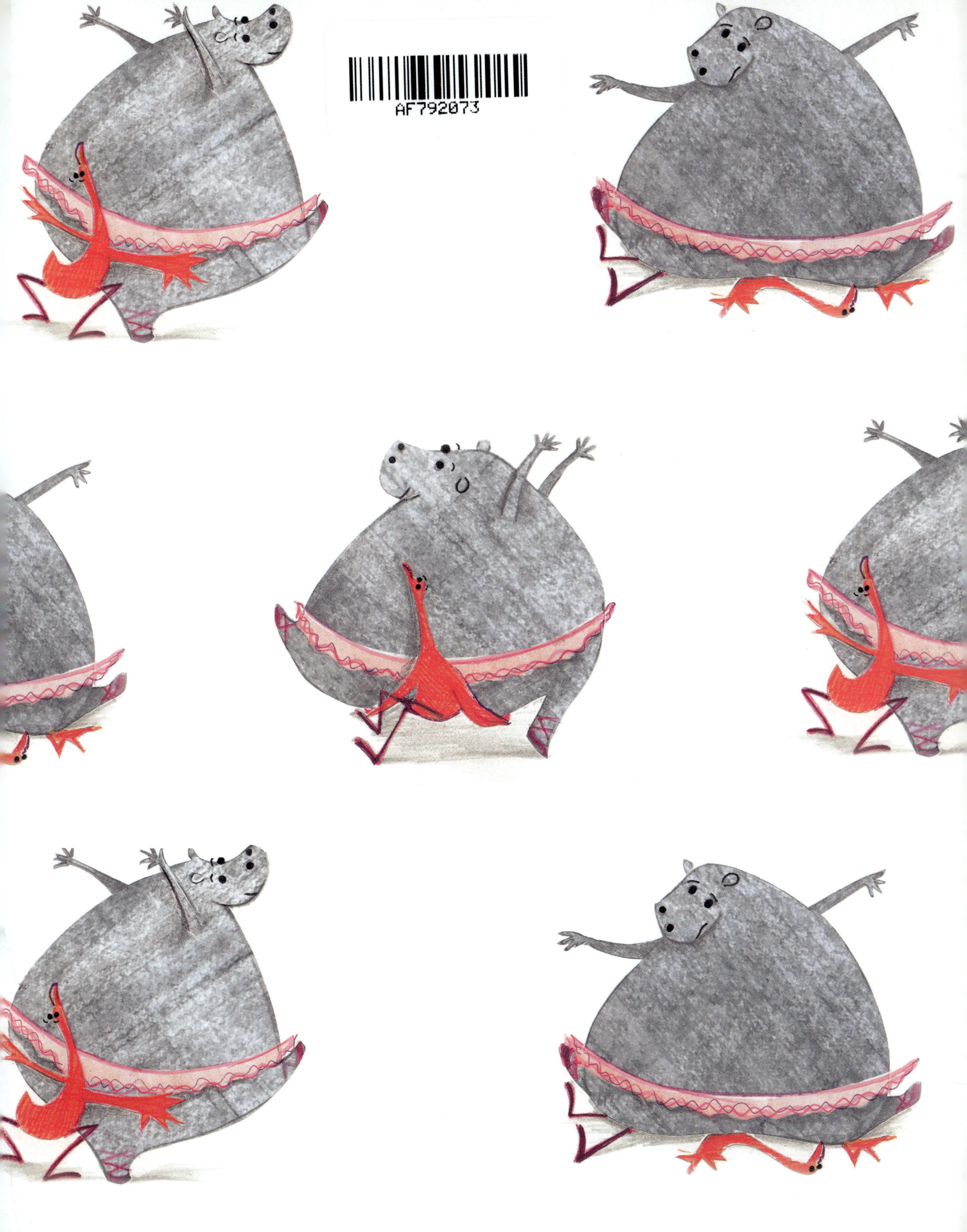

This edition published 2011 by Zero to Ten Ltd,
part of the Evans Publishing Group,
2A Portman Mansions,
Chiltern Street,
London, W1U 6NR

British Library Cataloguing in Publication Data
A CIP catalogue record for this book is available from the British Library

ISBN 9781840897128

Printed in Spain by Graphy Cems, Navarra

fiona

Hattie the Dancing Hippo

by Jillian Powell
and Emma Dodson

ZERO TO TEN

Hattie wanted to dance.

She tried ballet.

No-one could lift her.

She tried *ballroom*.

No-one would dance with her.

She tried tap...

...then jive.

“I’ll never be a dancer,” Hattie thought.

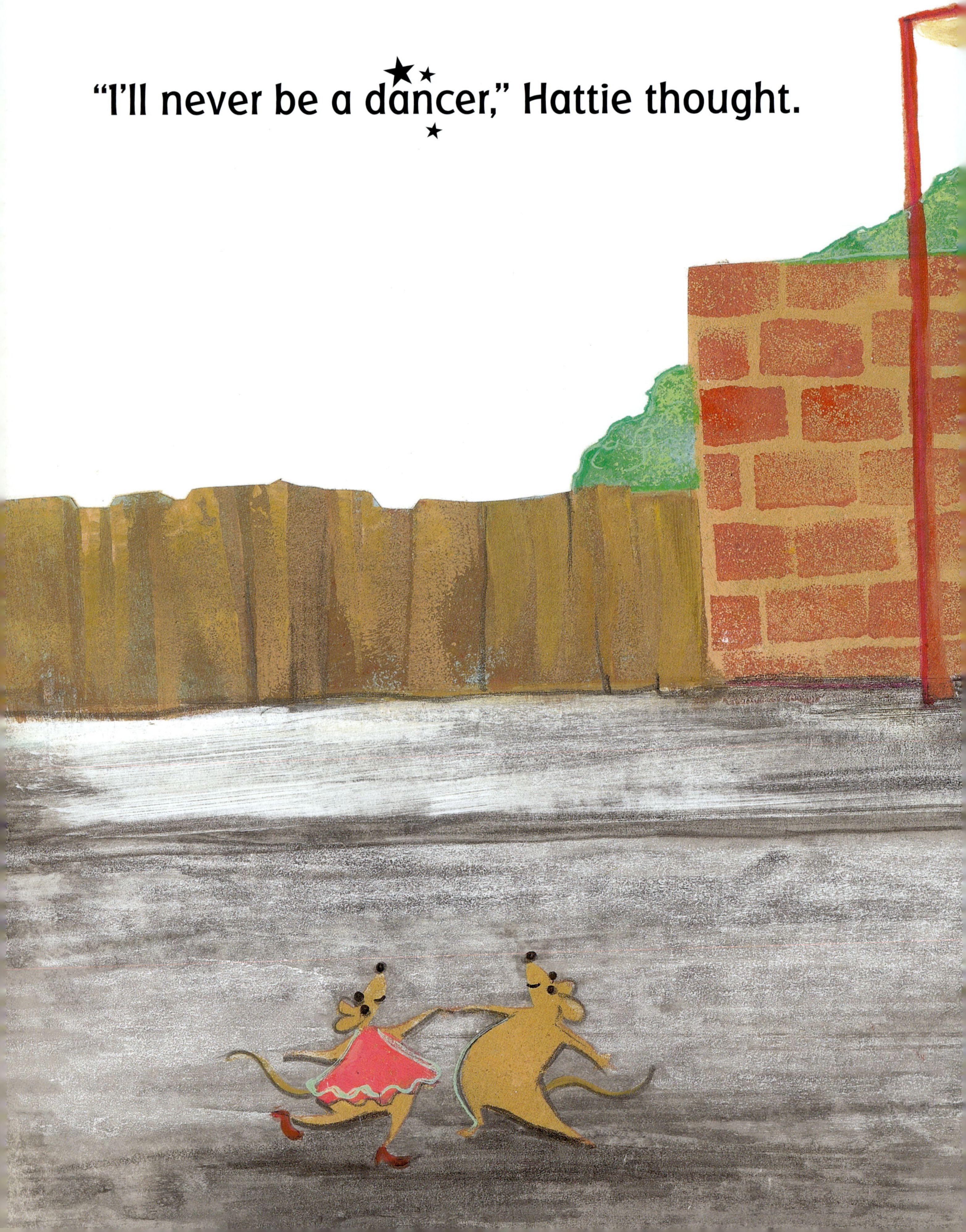

She tried one more class.

She wobbled.

She wiggled.

She waggled.

Hattie was belly-dancing.

She was the best in class!